Out You Go, Fear!

Mikaela Vincent

To my brave children
and to all who read this book...

Be free!

"Come on, Jimmy. It's time for bed."

"No! I don't want to!" Jimmy said.

"Why not, Jimmy? Don't you like the night?
        Don't you like when I turn out the light?
Don't you like to snuggle in bed?
        With the covers pulled way up to your head?

To see through the window
the moon's bright beam?
To sleep a sweet sleep
and dream a sweet dream?"

"No, I don't like it!
    I don't like it at all!
I'm afraid of the crack
    between my bed
        and the wall."

"Afraid of the crack?
    Well, we'll fix that.
We'll push your bed closer.
    And that's just that!"

"But Mommy, I'm scared.
    I don't like the night.
Please, *please*, Mommy,
    leave on the light?"

"Ah, Jimmy dear, there's nothing to fear.
        You know your Mom and Jesus are near.
Now get into bed. I'll turn out the light.
        Jimmy, don't be afraid of the night."

"But Mommy..."

"No buts. Now, listen to me.
        Whenever you're scared, just tell Fear to flee.
Jesus is with you. You're not alone.
        He will protect you as one of His own.
So sing Him a song that comes from your heart.
        Tell Fear to go, and he'll *have* to depart."

Scared little Jimmy
climbed into his bed,
and pulled all the covers
way up to his head.

His mommy kissed him
and told him good-night.
And then she went out . . .

...and *TURNED OUT THE LIGHT!*

The door shut. Clunk! And the dark closed in.
    A tingle started just under Jim's skin.

Wide-eyed, he peered out into the black,
    as goose bumps made their way up his back.

They tickled the nerves at the tip of his toes,
    and crept up his legs, his arms and his nose.

They itched at the top of his scalp, and then
    they stood all the hairs of his head up on end.

His shoulders shivered. His knees shook,
    as shapes shifted each corner and nook.

He watched shadows creep.
He watched them crawl.

He watched one make its way up his wall!

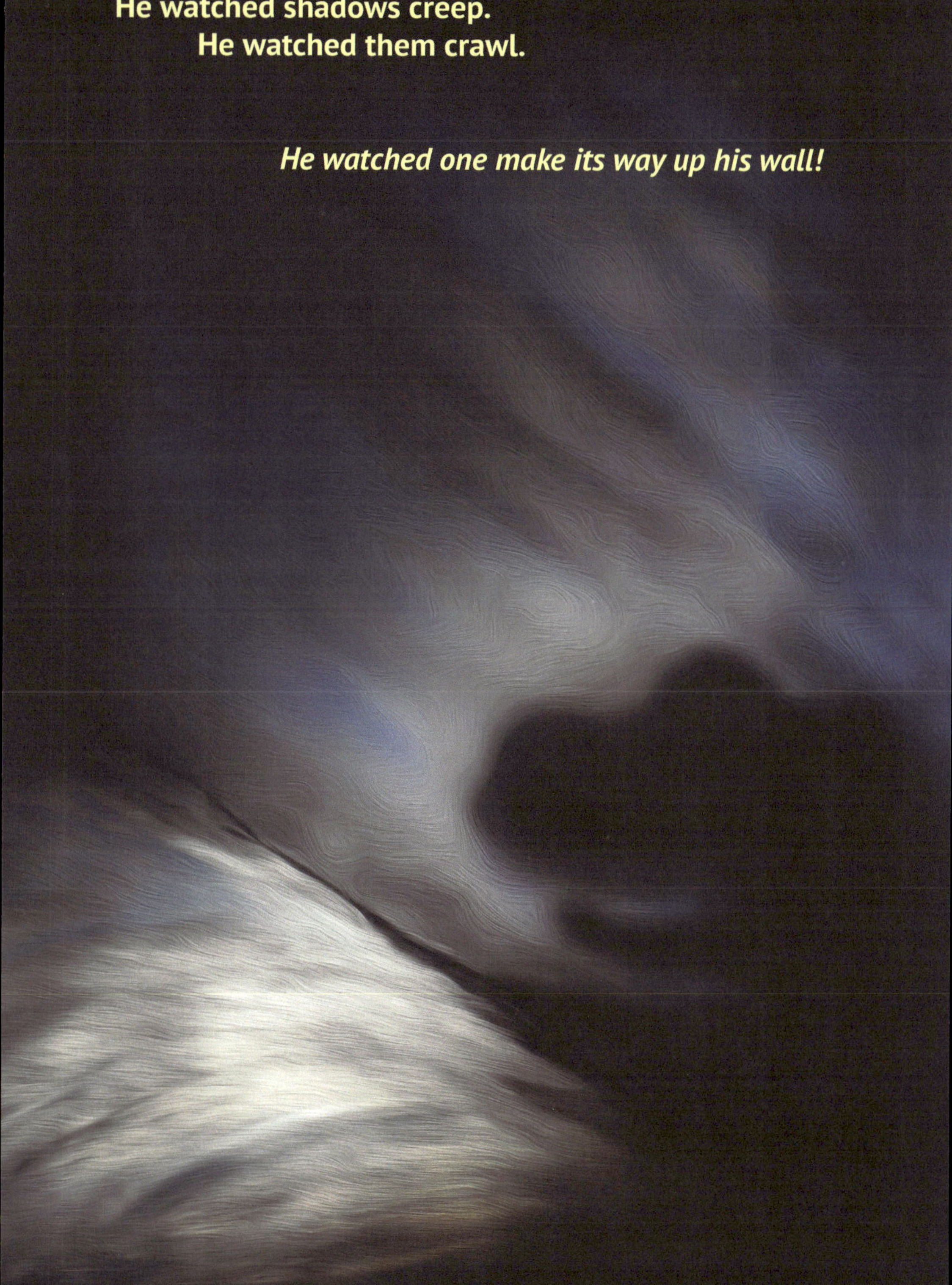

His body trembled.
  He heard his bed creak.
    Jim bit his lip
      so he wouldn't shriek.

He clutched at his blanket.
  He hugged tight his bear.
    He said to the shadow,

      "Who's that? Who's there?"

Fed by Jim's fright, Fear grew all the more.
It filled up the room from ceiling to floor.

For a moment, Jim froze, not sure what to do.
He forgot what his mom said; he forgot what is true.

Instead, he felt powerless
      there in the dark,
            like he couldn't cry out
                  and his dog wouldn't bark.

Like no one cared
      he was there all alone,
            helpless and hopeless
                  and scared to the bone.

He forgot to worship.
      He forgot to pray.
            He forgot what to think.
                  He forgot what to say.

He forgot that with Jesus
      he had the might
            to tell Fear to flee
                  and give *Fear* the fright!

All he could feel was
      trapped and afraid.
            All he could see was
                  the scene Fear had made.

He believed in his room
      was a foe so immense,
            it would reach out and grab him.
                  He'd have no defense!

With darkness and shadows,
      Fear lied and deceived.
            And all of Fear's lies
                  poor Jimmy believed.

But all of a sudden,
the truth Mom had said
came to his mind,
so he sat up in bed.

Despite what he felt, despite all his fear,
he wasn't alone. *Jesus was here!*

Choosing that truth, Jim said with a shout,

"**Fear, you're not welcome.
Now, *GET OUT!***"

Fear stopped in his tracks. "What's this? This is new!
Did little boy Jim just tell *me* what to do?"

"Yes. That's right. I said, *'GO AWAY!'*
In the name of Jesus, *you have to obey.*
This room is my room. My God rules here.
By the power of His love,

OUT YOU GO, Fear!"

Who trembled now? It wasn't young Jim.
No, *Fear* was the one now afraid of *him!*

With faith, hope and love alive in Jim's heart,
That creep had no chance. He *had* to depart.

As Jimmy began to sing a new song,
Fear covered his ears, and then he was *gone!*

"I love you," sang Jimmy, "my Jesus, my King.
I am Yours. You're my Everything.

Your love is so great, Fear has to flee.
But I know that my God will *never* leave me.

You're here in the night, when everything's black.
You even fill the space in this crack!

No matter the dark, Your love will still shine.
Please give me sweet dreams now
from Your heart to mine.

Send in Your angels to guard me tonight.
I trust in You, Jesus. *You* are my Light!"

When Jim worshipped God, Fear lost its hold.
Faith filled his heart where once Fear controlled.

That creep fled away and didn't come back,
though the night was still dark,
and the room was still black.

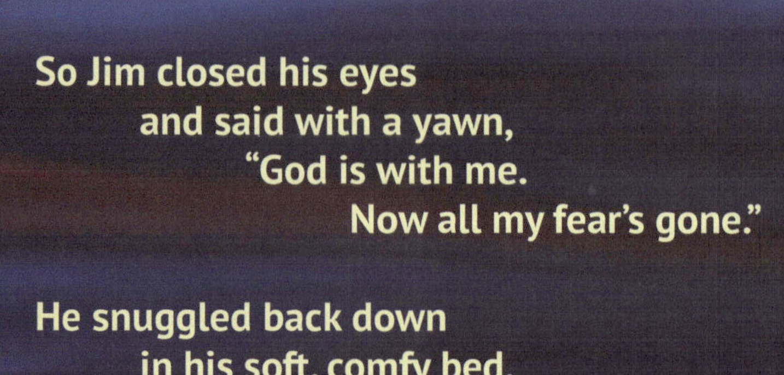

So Jim closed his eyes
and said with a yawn,
"God is with me.
Now all my fear's gone."

He snuggled back down
in his soft, comfy bed,
fluffed up his pillow
and laid down his head.

Happy and safe, Jim slept unaware
That angels had come because of his prayer.

Obeying commands from the King of all kings,
They watched over him and all of his things.

So, Jimmy slept soundly all through the night,
protected and loved by the One Who is Light.

And there in between
    Jimmy's wall and his bed
        stood the Light of the World
            with His hand on Jim's head,

Speaking to Jimmy
    in all his sweet dreams,
        filling them up
            with heavenly beams.

2 Timothy 1:7:

"For God has not given us
    a spirit of fear,

    But of POWER
    and of LOVE
    and of a sound mind."

1 John 4:18:

"There is no fear
    in love;

    But perfect love
        casts out fear."

John 8:12:

"I am the Light
    of the world.

He who follows Me
    shall not walk in darkness,

But have the Light of Life."

– Jesus

Sands of Surrender
Book 2: Chronicles of the Kingdom of Light

Banished to a desert and enslaved by creatures of darkness, Cory must come to terms with his past, as he battles a secret so high, so deep and so dark it threatens his very life.

Based on bedtime stories Mikaela created for her children, this second book in *The Chronicles of the Kingdom of Light* is an action-packed fantasy lit novel for older children, middle schoolers and youth (and any adults who dare!) that combines humor, adventure, and pure romance pure romance to help readers conquer lies and generational strongholds so the Truth will set them free.

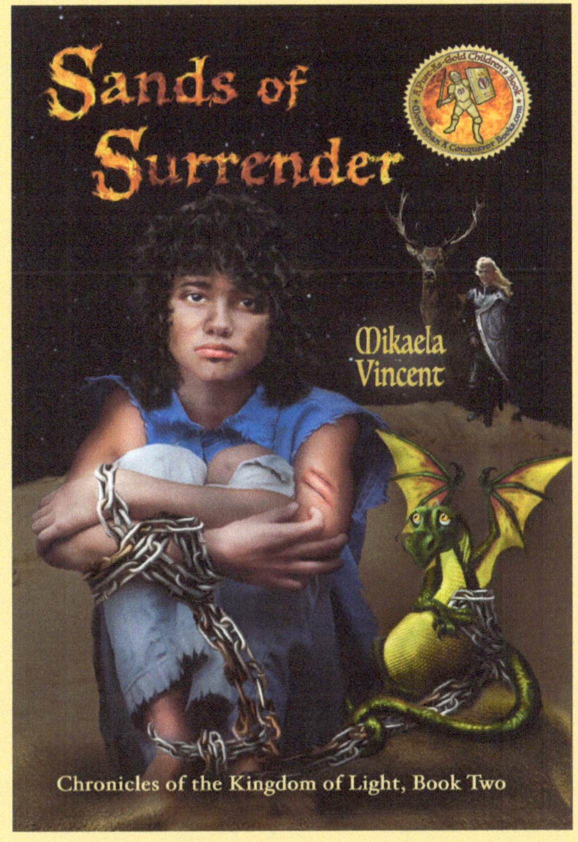

I Want to See Jesus!

This easy-to-read book for ages 4-7 uses colorful draw-ings and simple words to teach just-beginning readers that Jesus is always with us, even when we can't see Him.

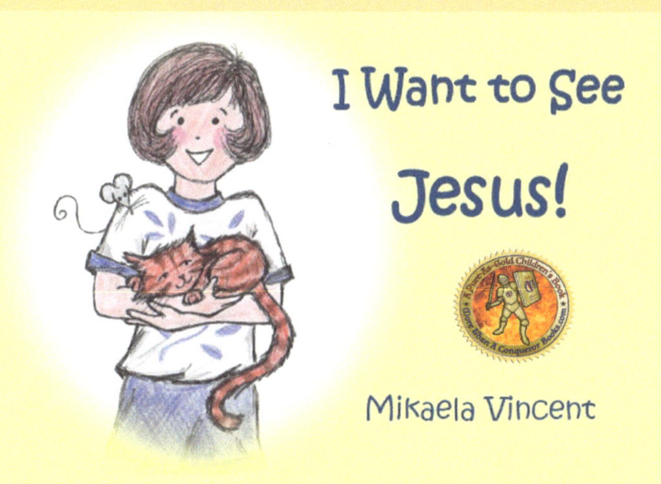

Also available in Spanish at www.MoreThanAConquerorBooks.com.

I Want a Horse!

Have you ever wanted something so much it was all you could think of or dream about?

In this inspirational picture book for ages 4-8, Mikaela Vincent uses colorful artwork, imaginative poetry and heart-warming humor to tell the story of a young girl who asks for her heart's desire only to discover a treasure she already has that surpasses imagination. Mothers and daughters will especially enjoy a deep bond reading together this fun interchange between an ambitious little girl and her wise and creative mother.

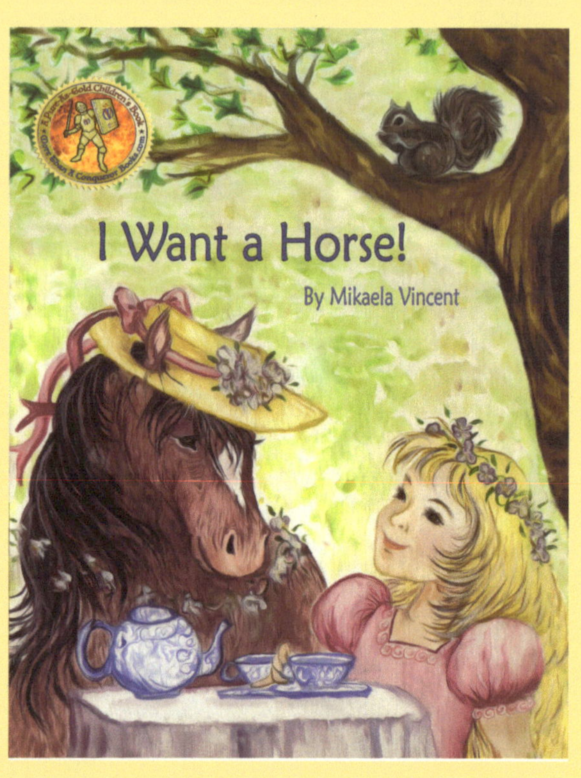

Delight to Become a Woman of God

It's not a fairy tale. It's true. You really are a princess destined to marry the King. You are beautiful beyond measure, and He is madly in love with you. Yes, *you!* And together you'll live happily forever after! It's all you ever dreamed life could be. And it's all yours, if you choose to become a woman of God.

Delight to Become a Woman of God features 30 devotionals from a mother's heart to her daughter's on drawing near to Christ and loving well.

.

Original illustrations, personal stories, thought-provoking questions, and sound Scripture all point young women to deeper depths with Christ, so He can set them free from the things that keep them from the abundant life they were created for.

This **Bible study workbook for middle schoolers** includes practical guides for knowing God's voice, going deeper in Him, finding a true prince, resolving conflict in relationships, and finding freedom from depression, loneliness, fear, anger, and other enemy traps that hold young women back from true love, peace, and joy.

Whether you study in your quiet times, together with your parents, or as a youth group Bible study, *Delight to Become a Woman of God* just might change your life! Leader's guide included.

Dare to Become a Man of God

Whether you like it or not, you are at war. Will you dare to defy enemy schemes? Will you dare to arm yourself to fight for the things that matter? Will you dare to walk in truth and purity, even when everyone around you is a prisoner of lies and sin? Will you dare to surrender your life to the King of Kings?

Dare to Become a Man of God is a workbook of 30 devotionals from a mother's heart to her son's on drawing near to Christ and living victoriously.

Filled with Scripture, thought-provoking questions and fun cartoons, this **Bible study workbook for middle schoolers** dares to make a difference in your life! Study it alone in your quiet times, together with your parents, or with other young men in your youth group. I dare you!

Leader's guide included.

All Vincent's books are availabe at www.MoreThanAConquerorBooks.com.

A note to those who don't yet know the Light of the World:

God created you for a purpose — to know Him, to worship Him, to enjoy Him, to feel His love and to love others through His love. He has a plan for your life, and it's a good one: "For I know the thoughts that I think toward you, says the Lord, thoughts of peace and not of evil, to give you a future and a hope. Then you will call upon Me and go and pray to Me, and I will listen to you. And you will seek Me and find Me, when you search for Me with all your heart." *Jeremiah 29:11-13.*

Jesus, God's Son, came to this earth to show us His Father's love and to offer us abundant life and forgiveness for sin if we believe in Him. But Satan wants to keep us from that life and entrap us with sin and lies (thought processes contrary to the truth in God's Word, the Bible). Fear is just one of those lies. John 3:16, 10:10, 2 Timothy 1:7, 1 John 4:18. When we believe Satan's lies and don't follow God's plans, our sin separates us from holy, perfect God. Romans 3:23.

But God loves us and made a way for us to be forgiven and reconciled to Him, not through anything we do to deserve it, but as a FREE gift. Romans 6:23, Ephesians 2:8-9. Jesus, God's sinless Son, died in our place to pay the price for our sin, and then rose from the dead three days later to show us His power over death. John 11:25, 1 Corinthians 15:51-57. The Bible says that if we believe in Jesus, God forgives us of our sins, we become His adopted sons and daughters, and we get to live with Him forever in heaven when we die. Romans 10:9.

Do you want to receive this free gift right now? To be forgiven, to know God's love, to let Him lead you through the hard times and give you joy and peace, and to know that heaven is yours? You can receive that gift now, and so can your child. Just pray a simple prayer from your heart like the one below:

> *"Dear God, thank You for sending Your Son Jesus to die for my sins and rise again so that I can have eternal life. Please forgive me for going my own way. I want to follow You now. Show me Your love, let me feel You close to me, and help me through Your love to also love others. Please set me free from fear and show me any other lies I'm believing that keep me from experiencing the fullness of Your love. I want to know You more. In Jesus' name I pray. Amen."*

If you have any questions or want to know more about God, please feel free to write me at MoreThanAConquerorBooks@gmail.com.

Love,
Mikaela

Teaching your children to listen to God

Read the Bible daily together.

During the first few years of your children's lives, they will lean on you like you lean on God. But around age 10-11 they will begin leaning on someone or something else. **It is vital for that Someone to be God.**

So, begin now, while their hearts are turned toward you, to read the Bible together with them and talk about ways to apply God's truth to their daily lives. Ask God to lead you to just the verses, devotions or Bible studies that are best for your family.

For our family, He asked us to begin with teaching them Bible verses using hand motions and songs when they were toddlers. And then as they started school, we began reading through the Word during breakfast every morning and talking about it together. We used a simple translation, read a few verses at a time, and asked them lots of questions. By the time they had graduated from high school, we had read through the whole Bible twice together.

Before we read the Word every morning, we prayed together, *"Lord, plant Your truth deep in our hearts so we can believe it and stand on it and walk out in it all the days of our lives."* To this day our children have said how impactful those daily family devotions were, because often God brought into their path opportunities to practice the truth they had just learned that morning. It formed who they are today as adults who love Him, make wise, loving decisions and follow His lead.

Listen to God together.

Every night, as you tuck your children into bed, talk with them about the events of their day, and pray with them, asking God to **fill their room with His presence and give them sweet dreams from His heart to theirs.**

But then, also spend some time just **listening to God.** Children have an amazing ability to see and hear the Lord because they don't yet have all the walls in their hearts that so many adults do. Lead your children to ask Him questions, like,

> *"Lord, when You look at me, what do You see?"*
>
> *"What do You want to say to me right now?"*
>
> *"Take me anywhere You want to take me and show me anything You want to show me."*
>
> *"Show me where You are and what You're doing right now."*

"What's on your heart today? What makes You happy? What makes You sad?"

After each question, give your children a time of silence to listen to God. And then ask them to share what He said or showed them.

This is a safe way to help them learn to recognize God's voice, because you are there with them and can check what they're "hearing" using this "Three-Fold Sieve" to make sure it's God speaking:

1. Does it line up with God's Word?
2. Does it line up with God's character, especially His love?
3. Does it draw you closer to God?

Another way to help your children listen to God is to lead them to ask God, *"Which character in this story am I most like and why? Where are You in this story and what are You saying or doing? What do You want to say to My heart through this story?"* Then read them a story from His Word and have them close their eyes, letting God paint the picture for them in their mind and heart as you read. Ask them to share with you what they experienced.

The stories about Jesus are the most fun to do this with, and it's best that you use the Bible itself, rather than a modified story. (Write MoreThanA-ConquerorBooks@gmail.com for suggestions on a age-appropriate translations.)

Model what you teach.

Get in the habit of listening to God in your own quiet times and as you walk through the day with Him. John 10:27. Run all your thoughts through the Three-Fold Sieve to make sure you're following Him and not your own ways or the enemy's. Proverbs 3:5-6, Isaiah 55:6-9.

Don't worry if you can't "hear" the Lord right away; just ask Him questions, position yourself to listen, and then look for His answers. He may use His Word, circumstances, others, or some other way to speak to you, rather than the way you're expecting Him to.

If you want your children to listen to God and follow His lead, let them see you pray before you make decisions, even the small ones you make all day long. Better yet, pray together with them, asking God what He wants to do.

And be humble. Don't be afraid to tell your children that you made a mistake or that you're still learning. That will give them courage to learn from their mistakes, as well.

Helping your children to freedom

Freedom from nightmares

The best protection against nightmares is to pray with your children every night for God to fill their room with His presence and His angels, to guard them from bad dreams, and to give them sweet dreams from His heart.

But if your child has a nightmare (or even if you do!), here is a wonderful method to open the door for healing and peace:

After some comforting words and hugs, invite your child to close her (his) eyes and ask Jesus to help her see herself in His arms. Then suggest she picture herself handing her dream to Him.

Ask her to tell Jesus how that dream made her feel, describing to Him the scariest parts.

As she is still in that memory, feeling what she felt when the night-mare happened, tell her to ask Jesus, " Lord, show me Your truth. What were You saying or doing? Take me anywhere You want to take me and show me anything You want to show me."

He may remind her of a verse, or even show up in the dream and fight for her. Once He has revealed His truth and love to her, her heart will be at peace.

When the hard things happen

The enemy doesn't play fair. He wants to plant lies in innocent chil-dren's hearts so they will act and react from out of strongholds instead of the Spirit's leading, perhaps even the rest of their lives. John 8:42-47.

Even you may not have escaped his schemes. Stop and think about it. When was the last time you felt angry, afraid, depressed, impatient, hurt, or anything else negative outside of the fruit of the Spirit in Galatians 5:22-23?

Ask the Lord, "When did that reaction/emotion/attitude first come into my life? Take me anywhere You want to take me and show me anything You want to show me."

He will most likely remind you of a memory from childhood when someone mistreaed you, or something else bad happened.

Stay in that memory with the Lord, remembering all the feelings you felt. Look for the lies the enemy planted, like, "No one cares," "I have to do this on my own," "I can't do anything right," "I'll never measure up," etc.

Now ask Jesus for His truth. "When that happened, Lord, where were You? What were You saying? What were You doing? Show me." Look around in your memory for Him or listen for what He's saying to your heart.

If what He shows you agrees with His Word and His character of love, drawing you closer to Him, then He may have just set you free from a stronghold by toppling enemy lies with His truth!

You can also lead your children through this process, only it may be much simpler and quicker for them.

For example, when our daughter was gripped with fear because so many people she loved had died in a short amount of time, we simply asked Jesus to take her anywhere He wanted to take her and show her any-thing He wanted to show her. He showed her one of those people she loved together with Him in heaven, and filled her with peace.

When several boys ganged up on our son to hit him, he actually looked for Jesus *during* the event. He saw Him leaning against a pillar, shaking His head and saying, "I told them not to do that, but they did it anyway. It'll be over soon, and then just forgive them." So, he did, and one of the boys was so touched he apologized; another eventually came to Christ because of the love shown that day. A couple of years later, I asked our son, "Remember when those boys...?" But he couldn't remember the event at all! That's how thorough his healing was.

So, as your child shares with you the trials he's going through from day to day, help him hand those feelings to Jesus and ask Him, "Where were You when that happened? What were You saying and doing?" Then give him time to listen.

If what he feels Jesus is showing him agrees with the Word and God's character of love, drawing him closer to the Lord, then his hear will be at peace. If he still feels something negative outside of the fruit of the Spirit, then just have him ask Jesus, "Is there anything else You want to say to me or anything else You want to show me?"

If you have any questions, please feel free to write me.

May you and your children be blessed and grow in the knowledge of God's great love for you! Ephesians 3:16-21.

Love,

Mikaela

MoreThanAConquerorBooks@gmail.com

Be free!
(Galatians 5:1)

Mikaela Vincent
More Than A Conqueror Books

We're not just about books. We're about books that
make a difference in the lives of those you care about.
www.MoreThanAConquerorBooks.com